Food ◆ Family ◆ Friends

What food you eat, whether your family nurtures or abuses you, and how friends fit into your life determine whether you live in despair or delight, cringing or cavorting through your days. F.I. Goldhaber's poems capture the marvelous and the malignant of all three.

As a reporter, editor, business writer, and marketing communications consultant, F.I. Goldhaber produced news stories, feature articles, essays, editorial columns, and reviews for newspapers, corporations, governments, and non-profits in five states. Now, her poetry, fiction, essays, and reviews appear in paper, electronic, and audio magazines, books, newspapers, calendars, anthologies, and street signs.

In addition, F.I. shares her words at events in the Willamette Valley, Seattle, and on the radio. She appeared at venues such as Wordstock, Oregon Literary Review, PDX SynesthiA, bookstores, libraries, and community colleges; gives presentations on subjects as diverse as marketing, writing erotica, and building volunteer organizations; and taught Introduction to Indie Publishing at Portland Community College and as a weekend intensive. http://goldhaber.net/poetry.php

F.I. Goldhaber

Food
Family
Friends

Feasting, flinching, frolicking through life.

Food ✦ Family ✦ Friends
Political Poetry Publishing
ISBN: 978-1-937839-27-7
All poems and photos
Copyright © 2017 by F.I. Goldhaber
Cover design by Joel Goldhaber
Copyright © 2017 by F.I. Goldhaber
Cover images from depositphotos.com

Political Poetry Publishing
an imprint of Fantastic Worlds Publishing
http://fantasticworldspublishing.com/home.php
P.O. Box 19963
Portland OR 97280

Table of Contents

Friends 51

Dedication

To all those with whom I've shared a meal, raised a glass. shed a tear, exchanged a hug ... l'chaim.

Food
Family
Friends

Feasting, flinching, frolicking through life.

Food

F.I. Goldhaber

Summer Market

Belly swelling with new life,
she wanders through the bright green,
orange, and white stalls. A cardboard
basket in hand, she savors
the sweetest tastes of summer.

Trickles of blackberry juice
escapes to paint her skin. The
baby's father licks it off
and his kiss offers her all
the promise of their future.

Berries

No look is quite as
triumphant as that of those
leaving the Farmer's
Market after scoring a
flat of spring's first strawberries.

Farmers' Market Bounty

The market's bounty flows across the kitchen counter
as bright colors emerge from cloth bags.

Orange peppers and tomatoes, yellow and purple
carrots, green lettuce, beans, cucumbers, squash.

Blue, black, ruby berries, luscious golden peaches,
white onions, brown potatoes, and red beets.

Pulled from the dirt, plucked from branches, picked from tall stalks
by gentle hands of those who love the land.

Spoiled by local abundance, it's difficult for
me to purchase produce picked by strangers.

So at the grocery store, while I may at times
indulge in exotic fruits, I avoid

The produce aisle. My cart looks so unwholesome with
only milk and cheese, packaged and baked goods.

But we often dine on big bowls filled with market
bounty tossed together with bits of cheese.

In winter, we fill our crockpot with roots and stems
that share flavors with a roast or chicken.

Many at the market know us and we inquire
about each other's health and wellbeing.

Although we don't garden, buying our food from its
producers brings us closer to the land.

F.I. Goldhaber

Distractions

As of old, the farmer's market
represents more than just a place
to purchase foodstuffs. The weekly
gathering buzzes with neighbors
greeting each other, musicians
playing, and even a poet
hawking his words to passersby.
But, I don't let the myriad
exchanges distract me from my
mission. Seeking only the best
of the best, I concentrate on
color, smell, texture, and firmness.
Lost in aromas and tactile
sensations, a salutation
from someone I know startles me.
Pleasantries exchanged, I return
to pursuit of most succulent
fruit and crispest vegetables.

Truffles

Rooted from damp earth
a little bit of heaven
sautéed for dinner.

F.I. Goldhaber

Autumn Harvest

Apples at market
bring both joy and sorrow for
their sweet crispness means
the end of summer's glory
and its bright, luscious bounty.

Winter Market

Hordes of Portlanders
starving for farm tastes
mob the winter market.

Blue sky gives lie to
our rainy season,
but vendors shiver in

the piercing cold. Piles
of rutabagas,
turnips, parsnips, carrots,

'taters, and onions
replace bright peppers,
tomatoes, peaches, and

berries of summer.
Kale and chard, instead
of lettuce and spinach,

keep displays green. The
sizzle of samples
cooking and enticing

aromas of soups,
pastries, crepes, and more
tempt shoppers to linger.

F.I. Goldhaber

Drive-Thru

I walk down the avenue,
drive-thrus lining the road on
either side. Coffee here in
myriad flavors, tacos,

fried chicken, hamburgers, dry
cleaning, pharmaceuticals,
donuts, and even money,
all available without

leaving their cars. SUVs,
sedans, and pickup trucks line
up six and ten deep spewing
fumes from fossil fuels and their

engines' heat that warm the globe.
They idle for a quarter
hour or more rather than just
park their cars and walk inside.

Fast Eating

The only thing fast
about fast food in
America is
the way it's eaten.
Sitting in the mall
food court, I watch one
woman inhale a
pretzel while she waits
in the McDonald's
line. People stop at
tables for only
moments to scarf down
pizza, ice cream, egg
rolls, fries, hot dogs. Then
they dart off searching
for more junk that
now resembled food.

F.I. Goldhaber

Seagulls

On the waterfront diners gorge themselves
on fish, oysters, shrimp, clams, prawns, and scallops
dredged in flour and deep fried to crispy gold.
Seagulls swirl about, clinging to the fence
screeching, begging for their share of bounty.
Sated on rich seafood, gull's natural fare,
diners amuse themselves watching terns
fight over potatoes and breading scraps.

Consumer Temple

Welcome to the warehouse, temple
of consumer excess. Fill your carts
with ten-pound boxes of sugar
cereal, hundred-pound bags of flour.
Batteries by the dozens; soap
in ten-gallon jugs too big to lift.
Enough food fills the shelves to feed
a small country, but it parades out
the doors for the SUVs to
swallow while shoppers waddle through the
exit sucking in pizza, ice
cream, and hot dogs too big for their buns.

F.I. Goldhaber

The Politics of Food

Have you ever known hunger?
Have you ever chosen to
feed a child instead of eat?
When did you last know aching
emptiness that lasted days?
Millions of children in the
U.S. go hungry daily,
many more throughout the world,
while billionaires steal the food
from their mouths to buy yachts, huge
mansions, fancy cars, private
jets, and their own Congressmen.
We subsidize the very
rich who eliminate jobs,
bust unions, ruin cities,
devastate education,
neglect infrastructure, and
take away our right to vote.
What they squander on one meal
at a fancy restaurant
could feed a poor family
of four for a month or more.
But, they begrudge the working
poor, the disabled, and the
unemployed whose jobs they stole,
the few hundred to spend at
a discount grocery store
to stop the rumbling in their
young children's empty bellies.

Forget about nutrition,
that's an unaffordable
luxury available
only to those deemed worthy:
those who got rich taking from
the public coffers, building
their wealth with government-paid
subsidies and government-
funded airports, roads, and ports.
They pocket their tax breaks and
complain about "handouts" and
nonexistent welfare queens.
Walk a few miles in a poor
man's shoes and skip eating for
a day or three. Try finding
a job when you're dizzy with
hunger. Give your meal to a
child who only eats at school
and goes without on weekends.

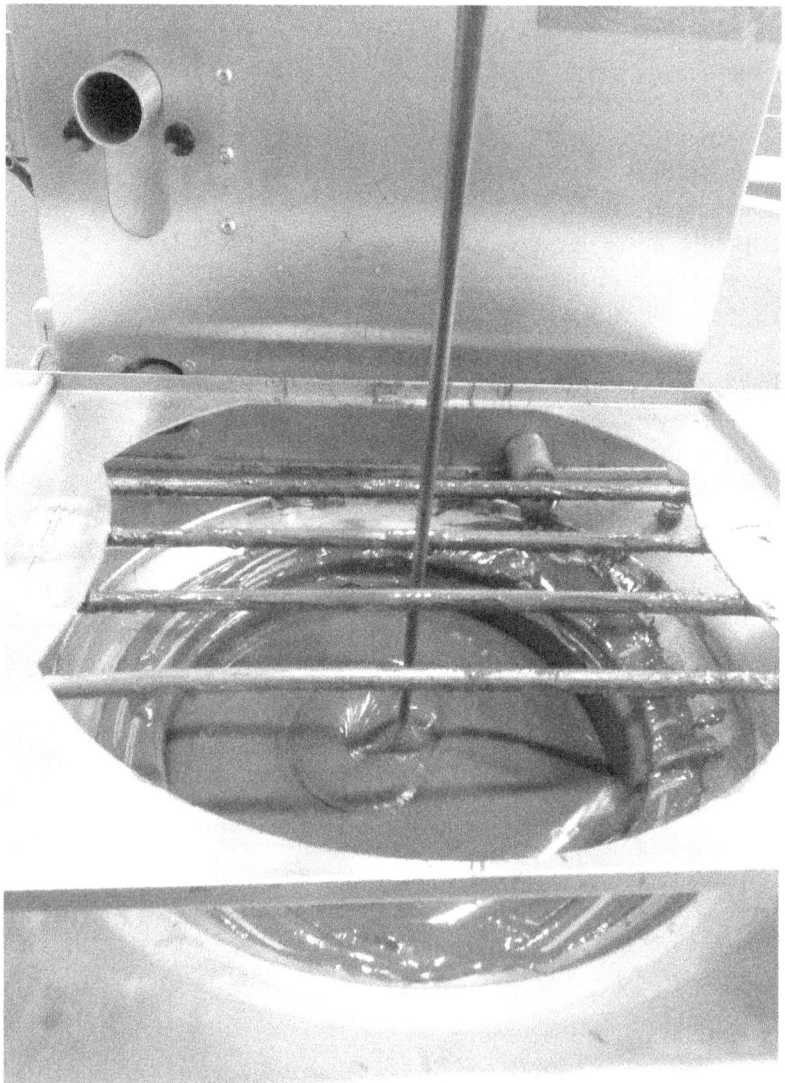

Ode to Chocolate

Dark, rich, smooth, and creamy
decadent concoction.
Elixir of the gods.
Treasured gift for lovers.
You melt on my tongue and
Feed the depths of my soul.
Truffles, ganache, brownies,
in every form you charm.
Even lighter potions
such as mousse and fondant
please my picky palate.
But, never milk. And do
not even mention white.
More cocoa, less sugar
makes you delectable.
Too chocolatie? I don't
understand what that means?

F.I. Goldhaber

Food Porn

At tables next to yours,
they whip out fancy phones
to photograph their food.
Before sampling even
a single bite, they post
their posh provender on
Twitter, Facebook, Flicker,
Instagram, competing
to prove culinary
chops. Does anyone care
about quality? Taste?

Filial Food

Pound after pound melted away, ounces at a time.
Desperate, unable to get him to eat, Mother
bought a train ticket for my culinary talents.
With butter and sugar, cheese and noodles, matzoth and
eggs, I resurrected rich memories. Two kinds of
kugel, chicken fried in butter, latkes, matzoth brei,
biscuits, lasagna. For a week I cooked nonstop, the
sloshing of the dishwasher my constant companion.
Each night I crawled into bed exhausted. But, he ate.
For the first time in a long time he enjoyed eating.
Ounce by ounce I added four whole pounds to his frail frame.
I left a freezer full of goodies and took delight
in Mother's daily progress reports. But not even
bubbe's recipes, prepared with his daughter's love, could
save him from cancer. Betrayed by his heart, snatched away
from the very many who adored him. So, we mourn.
We share the food that gave him pleasure in his last week
of a life lived long and well. His children, grandchildren,
widow toast his memory with the food of his youth.

Family

Cycle of Life

We
begin
our short lives
incontinent
unable to feed
ourselves. If we're lucky
we have loving parents to
fill our bellies, clean us up, sing
us a lullaby, and hold our hands.
We end life incontinent and
unable to feed ourselves.
If we're lucky we've
loving children
to clean us,
feed us,
care.

F.I. Goldhaber

Growing up Jewish in the American South

Pogroms and persecution are my heritage.
Violence and prejudice colored my childhood.
Forced, despite my protest, to say christian prayers
by people who refused to admit that Jesus
was a Jewish rabbi, just like my grandfather
at whom they threw stones and whose thick accent they mocked.

Both my name and my nose made assimilation
impossible in a culture unwilling to
accept anyone with a drop of blood that they
believed less than pure white. They created, where none
exist, artificial distinctions based on
skin color rather than accept commonalities.

Watching the prejudice and discrimination
meted out by those I considered my friends, once
boycotted by an entire neighborhood because
of whom we welcomed into our home, assaulted
and beaten for a creed I never practiced, I
grew up angry about injustice, bigotry.

As my lifetime stretches past the half-century
mark, I watch with dismay as the incremental
improvements of my early decades wash away
in the acrimony and hostility that
seem intrinsic to this one, much emanating
from the South I remember. I dread the future.

On the Fringes

I do not pretend to be white,
and there are those who would quickly
disabuse me of such a pretense.

I do not pretend to be black,
my ancestral skin long ago
lightened to more acceptable hues.

But, my world view was formed by the
neighborhood children throwing rocks
at my grandfather, by their white

parents boycotting all of us
for welcoming dark-skinned guests, by
the black girls who beat me up at
camp because of my heritage.

My life's journey takes me from
one state to another, never
staying long enough to plant roots.

While I may sometimes find myself
welcome for a bit among an
organization or small group,

at best I fit in awkwardly.
I've never belonged anywhere,
and I probably never will.

F.I. Goldhaber

Persecution

Five thousand seven hundred years
of genocide, holocaust, and
annihilation. Of exile,
wandering, and ruin.

My grandmother went to bed each
night not knowing if the Cossacks
would drag her out of it before
the morning sun rose.

My mother's parents ran from the
revolution. They'd thought with the
Czar dead oppression would end, but
pogroms continued.

My grandfather's family was
forced to leave their ancestral lands
while the British, Arabs, and Turks
bickered over it.

How many relatives I will
never know were massacred at
Treblinka, Auschwitz, Majdanek,
Belzec, Sobibor?

My people survived five thousand
years of oppression, injustice,
slaughter, displacement, and many
more atrocities.

Yet, aggrieved U.S. christians will
allege persecution if they're
not allowed to deprive others
of their civil rights.

They wail about the "war" on their
holiday, while expecting those
of every other faith to
to celebrate it.

This country caters to those who
call themselves christian, but like two-
year-old brats, if they cannot have
their way they cry foul.

Abused and Alone

Alone in the dark,
hoping the swelling
will subside and the
bruises will heal, that
blood will stop flowing
and your broken bones
will knit themselves back
together on their
own. Not waiting but
surviving. Living.
Longing for escape
even though you have
nowhere to run, no
place to hide, nothing
to spend for food or
clothing or shelter.

Haunted all your days
by the conviction,
planted in your mind
by perpetrators,
that you are to blame
for being abused.
Suffering from the
physical damage,
mental battering,
and emotional
repercussions for
the rest of your life.

Others ask why you
did not fight back, why
you did not stand up
to your abusers.
That victim blaming
just adds more shame to
your suffering and
preys on your anguish.

So you will spend your
life alone, taught from
childhood that you are
unworthy of love.

F.I. Goldhaber

Intervention

After studying
all the supposed
supernaturals
in which folks invest
their faith, I had found
none worthy except
her. A pragmatist,
I insisted on
seeing proof of her
existence with my
own eyes. I stood on
top Glastonbury
Tor to issue the
challenge and was not
surprised when she did
not answer. So, I
continued on my
lifetime path leading
to belief only
in what science can
prove and the good and
evil humans can
accomplish themselves.
Seven years later,
when it suits her, she
sends me one of her
own. A reward, he
says, for those good things
I've done or tried to
do to aid those who're
weak, abused, alone.
But she and a host
of others come with
him, and one by one
they reveal themselves.
One nudges me, I
sense a warrior's

34

presence, see glimpses
of another who's
hanging out downstairs.
I accept his faith
with his love. But, just
in case I waver
in acknowledging
their existence, they
send another who
walks with them into
my life. Wailing, "Why
me?" brings only the
reminder of my
request the divine
make herself known to
me. I'm told by my
love to: "Be careful
what you ask for."

F.I. Goldhaber

A Love Poem

"Get those ice cubes
away from me!"
former lovers said.

But you welcome
cold feet against
the warmth of your legs.

You sigh, content
to share your heat
with me as you share

everything else:
your heart, your thoughts,
your stories, your love.

Hallmark Holidays

Happy Mothers, Fathers,
Grandparents, Halloween,
Sweetest, Secretary's,
St. Patrick's, Boss's, Friends,
Groundhog, Valentine's day.

It's another Hallmark
holiday which you must
mark by spending money
on cards, decorations,
candies, presents, and more.

Keep the economy
going by spending your
money on your sweetheart,
parents, children, and boss.
Resist and you'll be ask:
"Where is your patriotism?"

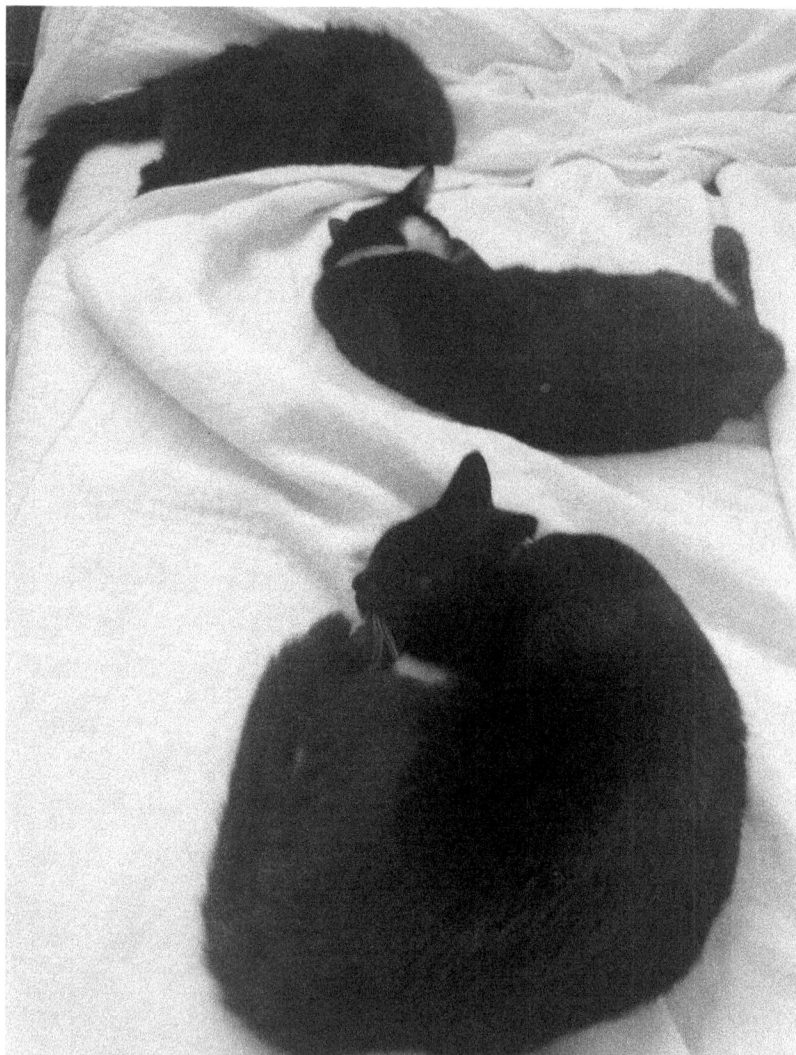

Full House

As the days grow colder,
one by one another
lump of fur crawls onto
the warm bed for the night.
We wake to a full house —
three cats o'er two humans.

F.I. Goldhaber

Conversations with My Mother's Purse

The phone jangles with their special ring.
I answer, hear her distant voice, but
can't make out her words. Thinking it a
bad connection, I hang up and call
back. No response. Now, I worry. Has
my father taken ill again? I
learn later, all is well. She had stuck
her earpiece in her purse, it turned on,
and re-dialed the last number called.

When it happens again, I hear the
unmistakable background beep of
medical monitoring machines.
This time I get an answer when I
call back. "Yes, Dad's in the hospital.
He may have had a heart attack, but
he's doing fine now." She'd planned to call
soon, to let me know. I wonder when
did the spirits start using cell phones?

Age Old Dilemma

I watch him shuffle along, hunched over
the aluminum frame that prevents falls.
His labored breathing and his twisted spine
slow his steps, trying his escort's patience.

I know I never want to live this way,
but, I'm too selfish to forgo his wit.
I won't let go as long as medical
science can keep him alive and walking.

I have no children to watch over me
when I reach his age, to make sure I eat,
drive me to doctors. But that also means
I've no one who'll need me to cling to life.

F.I. Goldhaber

The Master Gardener

All your life you took from the earth,
planting trees to feed you their fruits,
sowing seeds to reap succulent
vegetables shared with family, friends.
You grew dahlias, chrysanthemums,
roses — food for the spirit — to
delight your sweetie, make her smile.
You feasted from the bounty of
tomatoes, zucchini, onions,
greens, corn, beans, berries, plums, apples.
You coaxed every manner of fruits
and veggies from gardens planted
all over the country, and taught
myriad others how they could
enjoy a bountiful harvest.
Now we give you back to the earth.
We pour all that remains onto
the roots of a newly planted
red oak so you may nourish
it and help it grow tall and strong.
Soon, its acorns will feed birds and
rodents. The cycle continues.

The Urn

I search for the best display spot
for two inches filled with precious
memories from such a long life.
Lilith refuses to share space.
Stone and alabaster figures
of Bast and unknown deities
gathered from others' world journeys
withhold fitting sanctuary.
I turn to the five dragons who
menace from the most spacious ledge.
A fitting repository
for he who built rockets that sent
men into orbit, to the moon.

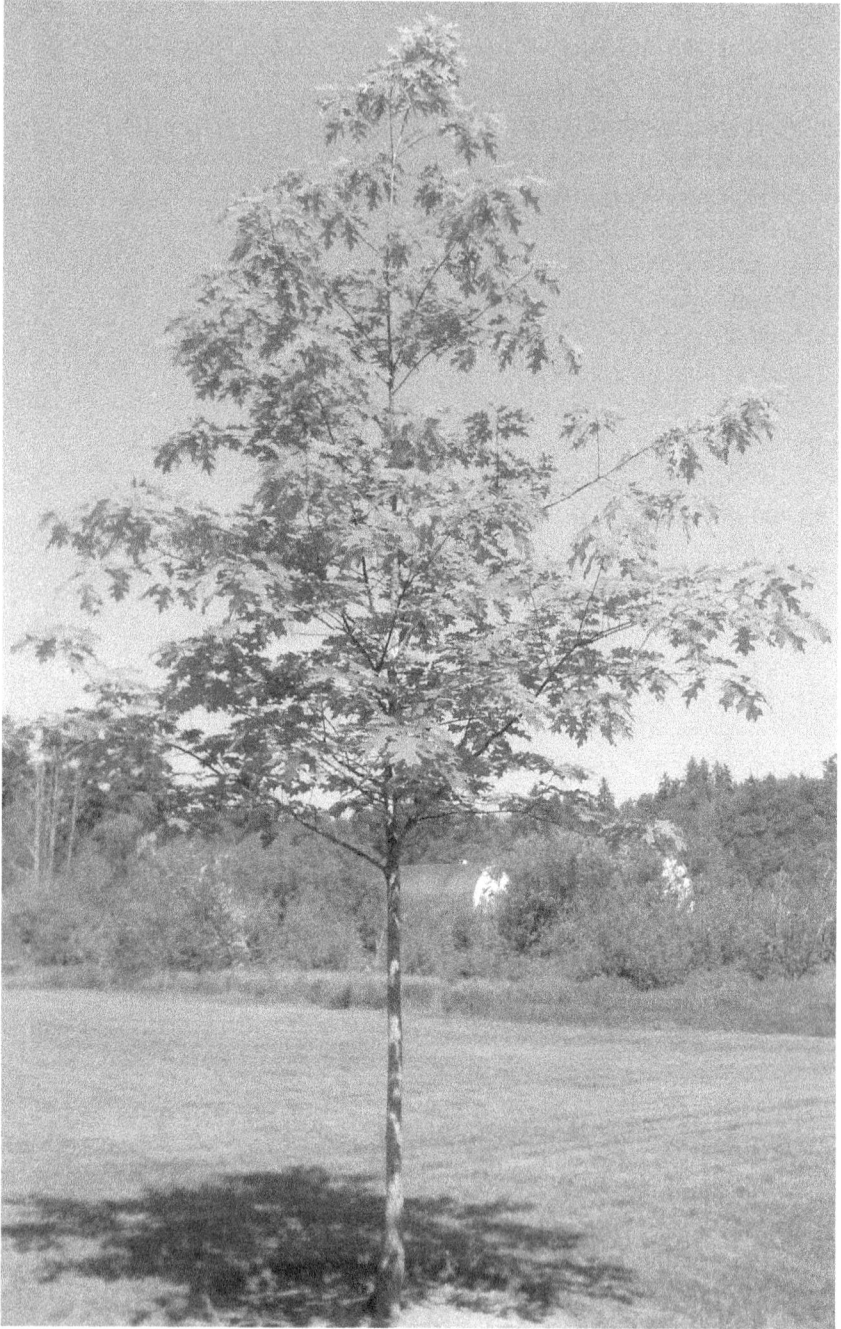

Kelsey Creek Shade

Two years after we
buried his ashes with the
roots of a sapling,
the shade of my father's oak
shelters us from summer's heat.

F.I. Goldhaber

You Are Not My Mother

Twisted with pain, cold to
the touch, only the whites
of your eyes visible.
You are not my mother.

Riddled with tumors, rib
broken, needles jutting
from bruised, paper-thin skin.
You are not my mother.

Gasping for breath between
long gaps, mouth so dry you
suck on the moistened sponge.
You are not my mother.

My mother walked for miles
each day up and down hills.
You don't move for hours on end.
You are not my mother.

My mother spoke about
politics, medicine.
You only cry in pain.
You are not my mother.

My mother gave me strength,
knowledge, understanding.
You can't say what you need.
You are not my mother.

My mother nursed patients
all across the country.
You require constant care.
You are not my mother.

We adjust your pillows,

cover you with blankets,
and hold your hand, but
you are not our mother.

You did not want to spend
your last days in a bed
plugged into machines, your
children watching you die.

I can't reconcile this
broken body with your
energy, life, and love.
I want my mother back.

F.I. Goldhaber

Ashes to Ashes

You went to nursing school to assure your independence
so you would never have to marry and let a husband
determine your life's course. But, before you graduated,
you met the man with whom you would spend the next sixty years.

Together you followed the rockets across the nation.
You cared for patients in numerous hospitals and
clinics, earned your license to practice in six different states.

You began when you were required to wear white caps and shoes.
You called doctors sir, all physicians were men, and women
only nurses, secretaries. Two degrees later, you
worked as a manager and doctors reported to you.

You raised three children, watched them struggle, find success, and wed,
then adored and spoiled your grandchildren into adulthood.
Retired, you spent decades traveling around the world.

Together you visited every continent and
almost every country. You traveled by ships big and
small, planes, trains, automobiles, and even an elephant.
You brought home myriad treasures, photos, and memories.

When death closed his eyes, you planted his ashes with an oak.
You visited his tree, watched him grow, brought him flowers, spoke
to him, and observed his leaves change colors with the seasons.

Now, we've mingled your ashes with his so you can always
stay together, nurturing this tree through many lifetimes,
offering shade to your grandchildren's grandchildren as well
as all those who come to this park to walk, run, picnic, and play.

Drops of Blood

At Passover, we dip our fingers in
the blood-red wine and drip drops on our plates,
one for each of the ten plagues.

We recite names in Hebrew: Dam for blood;
tzfardeah for frogs; kinim for lice; arov
for swarms; dever for the blight;
sh'chin for boils; barad for hail; arbeh
for locusts; choshech for darkness; makat
b'chorot for firstborn's death.

I no longer observe, but if I did,
instead I would name each drop for those I
have lost in the past three years:

My favorite aunt Sheila; my dear dad,
Jerome; his sister Toby; cats who
shared dozens of years with me.
Three friends who were much more: my colleague, Jay;
client, Connie; playmate Morgan; and now
my beloved mother, Bev.

Like wine dripping onto the Passover
plate, my strength, my youth, my love, my counsel
dribbles away from my life.

Friends

F.I. Goldhaber

Books

Shelves and shelves of books,
many stacked two deep,

line walls of each room.
Piles on the night stands,

stacks in bathrooms, strays
forgotten downstairs

where usually we
venture only to

eat or welcome guests.
Even the spirits

who haunt us love books.
They hide between the

volumes, then beg us
to acquire new ones.

At night we hear sounds
of turning pages.

The Conference

As I drive toward the airport once more,
a decade of memories rush at me.
I shed a tear for those who have passed, but
anticipate with delight embracing
the many friends I've made over the years.
Wise words will spill out into the hallways,
and excitement will permeate the air.
The exhilaration known only by
a writer who's been asked for more words will
drown out the airplane take offs. Rejections are
all too common elsewhere. But here we find
acceptance, support, and understanding.

F.I. Goldhaber

Seasons Greetings

Once upon a time, folks put pen to paper
to send messages of holiday cheer to
friends, acquaintances, family.

Then pre-printed cards made the task easier,
although most still wrote individual notes
and signed their names on the inside.

The days of photocopiers and bargain
home printers, allowed senders to insert
long, mass-produced, bragging letters.

As custom printing tech became less costly,
family photographs with a generic message
on the back became the standard.

Today the bragging is constant online with
myriad photographs posted of each meal,
excursion, and other "milestones."

Now randomly generated "cards" posted
on social media replace personal
greetings inked on linen paper.

Canvas

She's actually quite attractive,
in an unconventional way.
Her body's lean and shapely,
her art captures your gaze.

Metal decorates her ears, pierces
the cutis of her face and neck.
Vibrant ink covers her skin
with intricate designs.

You find it hard not to stare, but she'll
tell you "look all you want," taking
off her shirt to improve the
view. She loves sharing art.

Waiting

In the dark night I
pace the tracks, straining
to hear the whistle.

The sharp whistle of
the train that should have
arrived hours ago.

Wondering if the
boy even boarded
or I wait for naught.
The station's bright lights
beckon. But no one's
there. Only taxis.

Their engines run, and
cigarette smoke wafts
from drivers' windows.

I call the Amtrak
information line
for the sixteenth time.

F.I. Goldhaber

Bedroom Eyes

Do your eyes show her the window to your soul?
Or do they merely conceal quicksand to capture hers?

You promise she will stay in your thoughts as you travel.
It matters not, for she has banished you from hers.

She does not question your reasons for leaving,
but she cannot wait for your return.

Her needs overwhelm her, the need to touch to hold,
to sate the passion that churns always within her.

While you visit your warrior and fulfill family obligations,
she allows another to court her and win a place in her heart.

By the time you complete your journey,
she will belong to him and you will wonder why.

Barriers

You question the caution with
which I allow you to approach.
I have learned from the past.

You protest my base expectations,
"I'll treat you differently."
I keep my walls up.

You make promises, swear fealty,
beg the opportunity to prove me wrong.
You lie, even to yourself.

"Do not judge me by others," you cry.
"Give me a chance," you beg.
You do not exceed my expectations.

F.I. Goldhaber

True Love

The smile on your face
says it all, and I
treasure the look in
your eyes when you speak
of the woman half
a world away who
has captured your heart.

I know when you two
marry you'll come home
to visit even
less frequently than
before. But I'll let
your love's embers warm
me in your absence.

Fellow Travelers

You each have taken
different paths
to recognize
you cannot make the journey alone.
For a short while,
you have traveled
together the difficult road to recovery.

Some of you paid
a horrid price
because you did not
reach this understanding sooner.
Others suffered less,
but still see the abyss
that will swallow you if you can't learn new ways.

You helped each other
over rough
spots in the road.
Though now your paths part,
and you lose that support,
your spirits have intertwined.
You will never forget your time together.

F.I. Goldhaber

Tears

My heart is full of tears, but I can't cry.
Not for myself. My emotions drain
into my words and the characters I
write. For them I feel joy, pain, arousal.
For them I can smile, cheer, sob.

For myself, nothing.
I see the pain in my life, I just can't
weep for it. For I am the pillar of
tragedy and I must not weaken.

One friend had to quit her job.
She broke up with her boyfriend.
Another's lover betrayed her.
A third starts chemo next month.
A fourth is dying. A fifth just buried her son.
A sixth talks to me of committing suicide.

All of them confide in me. I must promise
I will not share their pain with any other.
They all turn to me for advice,
for consolation, for strength.
If I show my weakness, I can't bolster them.

My characters bring tears to my eyes,
laughter to my throat, softness to my thoughts.
But the fortitude I offer my friends
drains away my capacity to
experience my own emotions.

My heart is full of tears, but I cannot cry.

I Cry Alone

Their tears dampen the
fabric of my shirt.
I will wrap my arms
around their shoulders,
stroke their hair, help them
all work through their grief.

When someone breaks my
heart, I cry alone.
I won't share my pain
because that makes me
seem vulnerable.
I hide my wounds, my

tears wet only my
pillow. I'll not let
even he who caused
my distress learn he
pierced my defenses.
So, I cry alone.

F.I. Goldhaber

Tragedy

The headlines screech of
tragedy, the new
bride left to mourn.

Freak accident kills
three tourists, halfway
across the globe.

Two Americans,
tsk, we're meant to say.
How very sad.

No names mentioned in
the brief blurb, so I
don't learn until

weeks later that his
mother is a friend
of mine. Small world.

Death Watch

Word comes that one friend finally succumbed
to cancer as we prepare to leave for
the hospital to visit another.

One friend died last year. Two others had brain
surgery a week apart. And one won't
even let me know how she is doing.

None of the fearful vitriol others
spew about cancer feels appropriate.
My anger erupts at America.

U.S. medical inequality
allows one patient to gain eight awesome
years of living from radical treatment.

Another delays therapy she can't
afford. And a third gasps for breath, writhing
in pain because of cost-saving neglect.

Her history made annual testing
vital, but none was done. She suffered three
weeks from pain wrongly ascribed to a cold.

Why pay for a CAT scan when you can blame
her agony, caused by a tumor that
ruptured a rib, on strain from her coughing?

I see the daunting discrepancies in
treatment that my friends endure. I wince when
families trust their loved one's "in good hands."

For I know too well that facility
prefers to kill its patients rather than
pay for expensive care to save their lives.

And I rage at my own helplessness, my
inability to intervene, to
do more than offer succor, love, and food.

65

F.I. Goldhaber

Travels through Life

First name: my parents read to me. I begged for the same stories and poems over
and over then pretended to read them to my little brother with the book upside
down in my hands. I made up my own stories even before I learned to write.
My fifth grade teacher in Alabama encouraged the writer within and by high
school in Texas I knew I would make a career out of selling my words to the world.

Middle name: college in Washington offered discussions of Shakespeare as a feminist,
a course on human sexuality, and the one professor I still remember who spoke of how
words and music influence our culture. There I saw my first computer. Along the way
I abandoned my first name and started using my middle name until I discovered
I had two sets of friends who thought they knew two different people.

Initials: I started using initials to avoid gender bias, how many times have I explained this.
The calls came in for Mister and letters came addressed to Frank or Fred.
The woman in West Virginia, when told I had written the piece she called about,
exclaimed that I wrote like a man — from her a compliment. In the newsroom in Indiana,
some people started calling me by my initials instead of my name, and I liked it.

Still, I used my middle name most of the time. Started a business with
   initials on my card.
A chamber exec in Illinois declared my name a secret and I discovered
   value in that. I had two
identities — initials for business, name for personal — and two sets of
   friends who knew two
different people. Then I moved to a little town in Oregon — not big enough
   for both of me. My
initials found their way onto my driver's license and passport. No one here
   knows my name.

Other initials: Rabbis and scientists answer to my not so common last
   name.
When I started writing steamy stories I chose another name, and another set
   of initials.
At first no one knew who wrote those stories. But when I attend events
where I promote my erotica, I use the other initials and I've made many
   friends.
So now I've two sets of friends who think they know two different people.

F. G.

F.I. Goldhaber

Acknowledgments

The following poems have previously appeared in these publications:

- "Berries," "Truffles," "Autumn Harvest," on Portland Mall Management Inc.'s "Be Grateful" signs, posted on Portland, Oregon's transit mall, downtown.
- "Farmers' Market Bounty" in *Hillsdale Farmers' Market Grapevine.*
- "Winter Market," "Full House" in *Green Is The Color Of Winter*
- "Consumer Temple" in *protestpoems.org* and *Pairs of Poems.*
- "The Politics of Food" in *Subversive Verse.*
- "Ode to Chocolate" in *A Quiet Courage.*
- "Food Porn" in *TRN Literary Magazine.*
- "Filial Food" in *Survivor's Review.*
- "Cycle of Life" in *Icarus Down Review.*
- "Growing up Jewish in the American South" in *11/9: The Fall of American Democracy.*
- "On the Fringes" in *Fredericksburg Literary and Art Review.*
- "Intervention," "A Love Poem" in *Blue Hour Magazine.*
- "Conversations with my Mother's Purse" in *Gold Man Review.*
- "The Master Gardener," "The Urn" in *Bear the Pall: Stories & Poems about the Loss of a Parent.*
- "Kelsey Creek Shade" in *Windfall: A Journal of Poetry of Place.*
- "You Are Not My Mother" in *Connoisseurs of Suffering: Poetry for the Journey to Meaning.*
- "Ashes to Ashes" in *Soul-Lit: a journal of spiritual poetry.*
- "Books," "Canvas" in *Every Day Poets.*
- "The Conference" in *The Willamette Writer Newsletter.*
- "True Love" in *Long Story Short* and *Blue Hour Magazine.*
- "Waiting" in *Long Story Short* and *Pairs of Poems.*
- "Bedroom Eyes" in *Bridges to Nowhere.*
- "Barriers" in *Bridges to Nowhere* and *Love & Ensuing Madness.*
- "Tears," "I Cry Alone," "Tragedy," "Drive-Thru" in *Pairs of Poems.*
- "Fellow Travelers" in *Bridges to Nowhere, Humdinger Literary E-zine, Pairs of Poems.*
- "Travels Through Life" in *Diverse Voices Quarterly.*

68

www.ingramcontent.com/pod-product-compliance
Lightning Source LLC
Chambersburg PA
CBHW060141050426
42448CB00010B/2241